Wisdom for Grads

Boyd Bailey

Cover designed by truth in advertising
© 2014 Wisdom Hunters, LLC
Published by Wisdom Hunters, LLC
http://www.wisdomhunters.com
Book ISBN: 978-0615827162

INTRODUCTION

Transitions are hard, even good ones. These movements through life are tests to see how we respond to temptation and to examine the reality of our faith. Even students who are prayed for, raised well and have the benefit of parents who are good models of faith, love and accountability, can still stumble in the process of becoming a bold believer.

Graduation is a portal into the vast web of living life. You graduate from high school into college. You graduate from mom washing your laundry—to you learning how to iron and fold clothes. You graduate from meals miraculously arriving on the table at dinner—to your afterthought of throwing a semi-healthy frozen dinner in the microwave.

You graduate from a large home that is cleaned for you—to a small room that you are responsible to clean and declutter. You graduate from dad's cash coming just when it's needed—to you looking for odd jobs to supplement your spartan existence. Mostly, you graduate from assuming your parent's faith—to assuming your own faith.

Graduation is the ultimate transition, because it seems to come all at once like an avalanche over hikers traversing the Himalayas. Fortunately, there are the time-tested priorities of God first, family second and school and work third. This allows any sincere seeking soul to find and follow the Lord's purpose and plan for their life.

But, this intentional living does not come by accident; rather, it's through prayer, meditation on Scripture, wise mentors and a disciplined focus on following Christ. It is tempting to ask Jesus to follow us, instead of humbly submitting to and following Him. He has the right path that takes us to His place of peace, security and adventure. The wise follow Jesus, because no one else has the personalized purpose for living your life.

In a moment of doubt, a disciple of Jesus understood the need for Jesus alone, "Simon Peter answered him, 'Lord, to whom shall we go? You have the words of eternal life. We have come to believe and to know that you are the Holy One of God'" (John 6:68-69).

What is your source of wisdom as you embark on your tour through life? Like the Bible, does it have a proven track record? Or, is it servant to unpredictable circumstances and to the opinions of people—some of which fall into the very foolish category. Choose the reliable compass of faith and direction from Christ, and you will be much the wiser.

A life lived well leans heavily into the Lord. It is a sign of strength not weakness. Indeed, God's economy does not track with the ups and downs of the stock market; rather, it tracks on the trajectory of trust, contentment, generosity, saving and wise spending. Wisdom begins and ends with the Lord Jesus Christ, so fear Him, love Him and serve Him. A life well spent wisely transitions through life loving people along the way.

"The fear of the LORD is the beginning of wisdom; all who follow His precepts have good understanding. To Him belongs eternal praise" (Psalm 111:10).

TABLE OF CONTENTS

1

Giant Opportunities

"The LORD said to Moses, 'Send some men to explore the land of Canaan, which I am giving to the Israelites....' Then Caleb silenced the people before Moses and said, 'We should go up and take possession of the land, for we can certainly do it.' But the men who had gone up with him said, 'We can't attack those people; they are stronger than we are.'"
Numbers 13:1a, 30-31

As we face life, we can be overwhelmed by its giant obstacles, or be inspired by its giant opportunities. Challenges and uncertainty tend to corrode our confidence. It is in the face of the unknown that we can move forward by faith, or backward in disbelief. What giant obstacles are you facing? How can your obstacles be converted into opportunities? Obstacles are stepping stones for obedient feet to follow.

Therefore, with aggressive patience, stay focused and you will eventually see some obstacles dissolve, and others transformed into treasures. Maybe a financial giant is looming large as an intimidating obstacle. If so, stay true to your integrity by not selectively suspending your core values for much needed results. Instead, remain faithful to wise stewardship and honesty, and the right results will follow at the right time. Trust God to use scary giants for His glory.

God orchestrates giant opportunities for His greater good. He told Moses that He was giving His children the promised land; all they had to do was show up and receive His gift. Giant opportunities do require faith, planning, perseverance and hard work, as the reward of obedience and trust in the Lord is enough. So how are you facing the giants in your life; as obstacles or opportunities? Leaders look and pray for opportunities, and then explore them with energy and enthusiasm.

Your relentless leadership inspires your family, friends and work associates to remain faithful and not freak out. Therefore, take the land of opportunity the Lord has given you. Difficult days and economic challenges are greater opportunities for God to get the glory. So be aggressive, increase your efforts, pound heaven in prayer and by faith receive what your Savior Jesus has already given you. Go after the giant opportunities.

The Bible says, "I can do all things through Him who strengthens me" (Philippians 4:13, NASB).

What giant obstacle can I trust God with to become an opportunity?

Related Readings: Joshua 14:6-8; Isaiah 41:10-16; Romans 8:31-37; Hebrews 11:33

2

God-Sized Goals

"Jesus replied, 'What is impossible with men is possible with God.'"
Luke 18:27

God-sized goals are meant to challenge our thinking and further our faith. These Holy Spirit inspired "big ideas" are crafted by our Creator to spur us on to good works and transformational living. God-sized goals make us uncomfortable at times. They are not guaranteed to happen, but they position us to pray more and believe in God better.

It is through prayerful planning and implementation that gigantic goals move from mere possibility to a more sure probability. Huge objectives are a hedge against mediocrity and a prod toward perfection. God-sized goals are given to govern your thinking, and determine your time, so you are intentional and focused on His big picture. Otherwise, you can drift around without a rudder of reality, destined for disappointment.

Best of all, God-sized goals get you to God. It is prayer and planning with significant progress that moves you from the realm of possibility to the place of probability. In most cases it is one man or woman's passion and focus that proves catalytic to the creation and execution of the goals. The leader looks failure in the eyes and extinguishes it by faith, wisdom and hard work, which are all wrapped around a skilled and unified team.

Christ-centered possibilities far outweigh man-centered probabilities. Perhaps you need to get away in solitude for several days and ask your Savior to sear your soul with His goals. Think out of the box of small belief, for the Lord is unlimited in His abilities and resources.

God-sized goals arrest your attention, adjust your attitude and accelerate your actions. So, prayerfully set great goals, and He will grow your character in the process, while influencing others for His glory. Trust Him to teach you the way; to show you with eyes of faith way beyond the bounds of your experience, for His plan will prevail.

The Bible says, "I know you can do all things; no plan of yours can be thwarted" (Job 42:2).

What goal is God giving me that I need to accept by faith and work hard towards its accomplishment?

Related Readings: Genesis 18:14; Jeremiah 32:17; Matthew 19:26; Ephesians 1:19-20

3

Mentor Young People

At the window of my house I looked out through the lattice. I saw among the simple,
I noticed among the young men, a youth who lacked judgment.
Proverbs 7:6-7

Most young people yearn for someone to invest time and wisdom in them. They know deep in their heart they need help to handle heartaches. Their naïve knowledge has yet to graduate them from the "school of hard knocks," so they need loving and wise instruction. Who in your circle of influence is a candidate for your caring attention? It may be a son or daughter, a colleague at work or a friend from church. God places people in our lives for a purpose.

Perhaps you prayerfully pursue a mentor relationship with a teachable young person. They can learn as much or more from your mistakes as from your wise choices. Mentors are not perfect, just wiser from failures and humbled by successes. Look around you and ask the Lord to lead you to a young person who may be edging in the wrong direction. Reach out, and you will have returned the favor to someone who loved you.

Indeed mentors take time for others, because they are eternally grateful for those who took time for them. Gratitude to God is a great reason to go the extra mile with someone younger. Read books together, maybe a book a month for a year. Meet over coffee to discuss how the book challenged your thinking and changed your behavior for the better.

A young leader can preclude problems when he or she is able to model the wise habits of their mentor. Always invite an older adult into your life who can educate you in the ways of God. Moreover, the mentor process is valuable to both parties. It provides accountability, encouragement, love and obedience to Christ's commands. Mentor young people so they follow the right path, and in turn help someone else do the same.

The Bible says, "... Encourage the young women to love their husbands, to love their children.... Likewise urge the young men to be sensible..." (Titus 2:4, 6).

With what young person in my life is the Lord leading me to invest time, wisdom and resources?

Related Readings: Job 32:6; Psalm 119:9; Matthew 28:20; Titus 2:1-8

4

False Spirituality

"She took hold of him and kissed him and with a brazen face she said:
'I have fellowship offerings at home; today I fulfilled my vows.'"
Proverbs 7:13-14

Unfortunately, there are those who use religion to get their way. It may be a single adult who preys on an unsuspecting single adult in church. They attend church to take advantage of trusting souls. Some businessmen use the art of Christian conversation to give the appearance of values and principles based on the Bible. However, once they make the sale or close the deal, their self-serving and dishonest ways reveal them.

One of the worst types of deception is spiritual deception, because it is using God to get our way. In marriage it may be the husband who uses submission to control his wife, or a wife who uses grace to withhold from her husband. Therefore, warn those not to be like Simon in the early church, who tried to buy the Holy Spirit for his benefit. Cultivate authentic spirituality in your heart and mind through prayer, worship and community.

True spirituality, on the other hand, is motivated and controlled by the Spirit of Christ. There is authenticity because Almighty God is the initiator. True spirituality is not just looking out for itself but is sincerely concerned with serving others. You are comfortable with them, because you know they care for you. Integrity flows from their business and religious activities. Their yes is their yes, and their no is their no.

There are no surprises, because what you see is what you get. True spirituality comes over time, forged on the anvil of adversity, taught at the hearth of humility and received at the gate of God's grace. You know your religion is real when you love others above your needs, and you care for the poor and needy.

The Bible says, "This is pure and undefiled religion in the sight of our God and Father, to visit orphans and widows in their distress, and to keep oneself unstained by the world" (James 1:27, NASB).

Who do I need to confront in love about using their "Christianity" to take advantage of others?

Related Readings: Ecclesiastes 7:4; Matthew 25:36; Acts 8:19-20; 2 Corinthians 1:17

5

Pay Attention

Now then, my sons, listen to me; pay attention to what I say.
Proverbs 7:24

Pay attention, because there are some people who want to help you, and some who want to hurt you. Especially pay attention to those who seem to say the right things, but in their heart they have a hidden agenda. Everyone cannot be trusted, because not everyone is trustworthy. The sooner you discern a man or woman's motive, the quicker you will know how to manage your time.

If in conversation it is all about them, then watch out for wrong behavior. Pay attention to the path people may want you to take and so protect your reputation. Moreover, you have limited emotional capacity and mindshare, so make sure the Lord is leading you to get involved. Even good people and compelling causes can lead you astray. Pay attention, and learn to say no, so you can say yes to God's best.

I struggle with saying no, because I want to please people. However, pleasing people is not the best motivation. Faith in my Heavenly Father is a much nobler goal. Learning to say no is how we gain peace and contentment over the long haul. When you say no to someone or something, you can trust your Savior Jesus to take care of the need, and to take care of you. Your no opens the door for someone else to be blessed by their yes.

In some cases saying no requires more faith than saying yes. Therefore, pay attention and be prayerful, before you commit time and resources. Certainly as you encounter temptation, do not entertain the slightest hint of yes. It is better to say no to his or her advances, and lose a friendship, than to say yes, and lose your good name and gain regret. Pay attention and say no to earthly impulses, so you can say yes to heaven's best.

The Bible says, "Set your minds on things above, not on earthly things" (Colossians 3:2).

In what area of my life do I need to pay more attention, and say no more often?

Related Readings: 2 Chronicles 20:15; Psalm 34:11; Mark 7:14; 1 Corinthians 4:14-15

6

Wisdom Speaks Out

Does not wisdom call out? Does not understanding raise her voice?
On the heights along the way, where the paths meet, she takes her stand...
Proverbs 8:1-2

Wisdom is not shy, it proclaims itself and speaks out in public places. Like the Lord speaking to Moses on Mt. Sinai: He spoke wisdom loudly with authority, clarity and finality. Like John the Baptist, who boldly cried out to the crowds for repentance and faith in Christ. Wisdom is not a secret, secluded in solitary confinement waiting to be let out. It calls out publicly and openly.

Because wisdom is so easily accessible, it is imperative we listen and learn from its instruction. Sunday morning teaching at your church should be a reservoir of wisdom. If not, consider transferring to a fellowship where access to truth is easy to find. Wisdom drowns out the whispers of gossiping fools, because wisdom has the last word. Listen for wisdom and you will learn how to follow the Lord.

The way of wisdom works, because it invites God's blessing. For example, financial wisdom is to avoid debt, save up and pay cash. Relational wisdom is to listen with understanding to another's needs, say back what you heard to confirm your comprehension and, if appropriate, offer ideas that may bring benefit. Parenting wisdom is to find couples whose children are upright, and learn from them.

Business wisdom is to build your enterprise on honesty and integrity; do not compromise your convictions for cash. Wisdom has worthy things to say, so each day listen for it and learn. Train your ears to listen for wisdom in sermons and everyday conversations. Expose your eyes to wisdom in books and the Bible. Lastly, look for wise behavior to emanate from those who enjoy the fruit of faithful living. Wisdom speaks out, so you can live it out.

The Bible says, "Wisdom shouts in the street, she lifts her voice in the square" (Proverbs 1:20).

Where is wisdom trying to get my attention, and how can I apply its truth?

Related Readings: Exodus 19; Isaiah 58:1; Matthew 3:3; John 7:37; Hebrews 12:25

7

Hate Evil

To fear the Lord is to hate evil; I hate pride and arrogance,
evil behavior and perverse speech.
Proverbs 8:13

The word hate makes us uncomfortable. It has a harsh and uncaring ring and reputation. However, there is a holy hatred of evil that is allowed by Almighty God and even expected. Authentic Christianity is not easy on evil, because it breaks the heart of God and destroys the soul of man. Evil is an encroachment by the enemy on eternity's agenda. It takes down leaders who let pride and arrogance seep into their thick skulls and stay there.

Indeed, if the rules apply to everyone but the leader, then it's just a matter of time before the fear of the Lord becomes a foreign concept. Sin is out of bounds for any child of God that abounds in the love and grace of God. It is the wisdom of Christ that warms the heart, instructs the mind and leads the way into behavior defined by truth. The Bible says, "God's mystery, that is, Christ Himself, in whom is hidden all treasures of wisdom and knowledge" (Colossians 2:2b-3, NASB).

Gossip, greed, jealousy and lies are all evil intentions that corrupt a culture of transparency, generosity, contentment and honesty. Stress can bring out the best and worst in others, so make sure by the grace of God that you rise above the petty politics of blame. Wisdom and maturity take responsibility and seek to lead the team in excellent execution of a proven strategy. If you do nothing, then the naysayers will negotiate for fear and division.

Furthermore, fight evil without fanfare, but by faith and wise work deliver constant and creditable results, and your antagonists will grow quiet. It is the humility and wisdom of Christ that defeats evil initiatives. Therefore, give Him the glory, get the job done and trust the Lord with the results. Hard times can produce hard hearts, unless you overcome evil with a humble heart of prayer and bold faith. Evil is extinguished under intense intercession of prayers from pure people.

The Bible says, "Make this your common practice: Confess your sins to each other and pray for each other so that you can live together whole and healed. The prayer of a person living right with God is something powerful to be reckoned with" (James 5:16, The Message).

What does a holy hatred of evil look like in my life?

Related Readings: Amos 5:15; Zechariah 8:17; Romans 12:9; 2 Timothy 2:19

8

Timely Transitions

The rest of their brothers (the priests and the Levites and all who had returned
from the captivity to Jerusalem) began the work, appointing Levites twenty
years of age and older to supervise the building of the house of the Lord.

Ezra 3:8b

Transitions are hard, even good ones. But sometimes it is time to move out and to move on. God may be calling you back to a particular city or town for you to influence old and new friends for Christ. Or, He may be calling you to a brand new endeavor full of wonder and risk. Either way, your transition is what is best for His kingdom and for your spiritual growth. Transitions are a time to trust totally and to live boldly. Yes, pray much and seek godly counsel, but do not let fear of the unknown stifle you. This life is your one opportunity to follow hard after God.

"Seek the LORD while he may be found; call on him while he is near" (Isaiah 55:6). Do not let the things of this world paralyze you, or cause you to pause. Hesitation can hurt. However—in your zeal—do be sensitive to your family. Make sure to nurture them through the process. Retain Christ as your compass through the transition. He will keep you honest and soften the hearts of those most affected by the move.

Transitions can be exciting. They can keep us young. They move our faith to a whole new level. You could have stayed in your comfort zone feeling a minimal need for God. But now your dependence on Him is daily, even real time. You feel and know He is your loving Heavenly Father. Your circumstances may or may not get better, but you will.

Is He leading you to a new city? Hire a realtor. Does He want you to downsize so you can simplify your life? Put up a for sale sign. Does He want you to reach out to your neighbor? Invite them to dinner. Does He want you to move overseas and train national leaders? Buy a passport.

Divinely orchestrated transitions are like a loyal friend, whom you totally trust. Ride change like the ocean waves. It may be a little scary—maybe a lot scary—but He is with you. You will crash occasionally—but He will buffer your fall—like resting on a soft sandy sea bottom. Let this transition lead you closer to God and His will. You will never know exactly what you would have missed if you don't, and you will have few regrets if you do.

"Keep your lives free from the love of money and be content with what you have, because God has said, 'Never will I leave you; never will I forsake you.' So we say with confidence, 'The Lord is my helper; I will not be afraid. What can man do to me?'" (Hebrews 13:5-6)

What transition do I need to embrace, celebrate and trust the Lord is with me?

Related Readings: Psalm 66:6; Isaiah 43:2; Acts 12:10; Hebrew 11:29

9

Rich Provision

Wisdom has built her house; she has hewn out its seven pillars.
She has prepared her meat and mixed her wine; she has also set her table.
Proverbs 9:1-2

Wisdom is the pathway to God's rich provision. His Holy Spirit allows you to see the common with uncommon eyes, and thus come up with creative alternatives. Wisdom is the Lord's way of preparing for you plenty of resources and relationships to further His will. He is not slack in sending forth His Holy Spirit, who provides discernment of people's motives and insights into situations.

Therefore, ask the Lord to help you understand what to do and what not to do. When God gives you the "green light," then go forward by faith knowing He will provide. He has prepared a place for you, not only in heaven, but also on earth. Wisdom's preparations are plentiful and pretty. So be patient, do the next wise thing and watch God work in ways you never imagined. Wisdom is at work on behalf of your work.

Maybe He is calling you to worship and community with different followers of Christ. A church built on the foundation of God's wisdom is the best preparation for your faith and family. Yes, you are best fed in a family of faith where the Word of God is given full attention and examination. Like the Bereans in the early church, you are encouraged to ask bold questions related to the meaning of Scripture.

The church is God's house for prayer and the proclamation of His principles for the gaining of wisdom needed to live life. Therefore, gather wisdom every chance you get and you will become rich indeed: rich in relationships, rich in character, rich in robust relationship with Jesus, and maybe rich in stuff. Wisdom is at work on your behalf, so tap into its rich provision.

The Bible says, "For every house is built by someone, but the builder of all things is God" (Hebrews 3:4).

How can I access by faith, the provision that wisdom is preparing for me?

Related Readings: Genesis 43:16; Acts 17:10-12; 1 Timothy 3:15; 1 Corinthians 3:9-15

10

God's Favor

Blessed is the man who listens to me [wisdom], watching daily at my doors, waiting at my doorway. For whoever finds me finds life and receives favor from the Lord.
Proverbs 8:34-35

God's favor is the fruit of friends who find wisdom. They seek wisdom by first watching at the doors of heaven and waiting patiently at the feet of their Savior Jesus. It is humbling to think each day Almighty God is available to commission our cause for Christ. The wisdom of Jesus is what we pursue, because His is pure and profound.

Like Abel, the Almighty looks for the best offering for blessing. Therefore, honor God by offering Him the first fruits of your day. Just as He deserves "first dibs" on your money, so He expects the beginning of your day. Get up and go to God first. There you discover a wealth of wisdom, and under the shadow of your Savior Jesus Christ you receive His favor.

Happiness happens to those who wait for wisdom. His blessing cannot be rushed, so rest in Him. The favor of God is absolutely worth the wait; like the arrival of a newborn, the joy is unspeakable. How many times have we rushed ahead outside the canopy of Christ's blessing? The Israelites learned to stay under the cloud of God and be lead by faith.

Indeed, there is no spiritual oxygen to sustain those in an "out of favor" environment. It is lifeless and lonely. However, for those on whom their Heavenly Father's favor rests, there is rest. His blessing provides strength for the journey, and perseverance to stay on the trail of trust. Jesus experienced the favor of His Heavenly Father when He submitted to public baptism (His confession of faith) and His commitment to public service (His commission to ministry).

On what issue of obedience do you need wisdom, so to continually experience the favor of your Heavenly Father? Your life is alive and vibrant, because the Lord favors you. You are a favorite of your Heavenly Father, because you are learning to wait on Him and to humbly walk with the wise.

The Bible says, "He has told you, O man, what is good; and what does the LORD require of you but to do justice, to love kindness, and to walk humbly with your God?" (Micah 6:8, NASB).

How can I make sure to stay "bless-able" and in a position to receive God's favor?

Related Readings: Genesis 4:4; Exodus 33:12; Luke 2:52; Philippians 3:8

11

Tempered Talk

When words are many, sin is not absent,
but he who holds his tongue is wise.
Proverbs 10:19

Tempered talk is evidence of wise conversation. It's when our words are many that we run the risk of soliciting sin. Increased words increase the probability of improper speech. For example, respectful conversation does not repeat over and over again the same words and phrases in a limited period of time. This inconsiderate cadence frustrates.

Perhaps a look of misunderstanding requires questions for clarification, or definitions for comprehension. Proud conversationalists can highjack a hearer's understanding with a hoard of words without meaning. If your goal is to communicate, then take the time to listen to the needs of your audience. People who feel cared for and understood have a keener sense of hearing and understanding. The Bible says, "Even a fool is thought wise if he keeps silent, and discerning if he holds his tongue" (Proverbs 17:28).

Wise people weigh their words before they speak. They allow their minds to catch up with their hearts. Furthermore, in the face of wrong behavior emotions need to sometimes express themselves. Let the other person know if you feel mistreated or misinformed. Concealed anger leads to living a lie (see Proverbs 10:18), but tempered talk is truthful and to the point.

Lastly, you reserve your words out of respect for the other person. If you do all the talking, you are the center of attention. It is condescending conversation, because the other individual does not feel important enough to speak up. So, you honor others when you speak less, and listen more intently for ways you can love them. Wisdom can be found in the words of each person you meet. Therefore, intentionally talk less and be wise.

The Bible says, "My dear brothers, take note of this: Everyone should be quick to listen, slow to speak and slow to become angry" (James 1:19).

To whom should I listen more and talk less?

Related Readings: Job 2:3; Amos 5:13; Titus 1:10; James 3:2

12

Righteous Resolve

The righteous will never be uprooted, but the wicked will not remain in the land.
Proverbs 10:30

Resolve is the result of righteous living. There is a determination deep within a soul dependent on God. When you are established in the faith, no one can remove you from Christ's call. He has appointed you to this post of service. Do not leave until the Lord reassigns you. Righteous resolve decides to stay put; so by faith, keep on for Christ.

It probably means you disappoint some and invigorate others. However, if your goal is to first trust and obey the Lord, you will be misunderstood by some and rejected by others. Friends may even urge you to move on, but you cannot because Christ has not released you. Your resolve is His resolve. Therefore, you persevere through pain, suffering and uncertainty. Righteous resolve remains, regardless of the consequences, good or bad.

Moreover, there is a righteous resolve that remains in Christ (see John 15:5). Your conversion to Christianity was a resolution to abide under the influence of Almighty God. You stay true to your commitment to Christ because of the joy that comes from following Jesus. The "meek inherit the earth" (Matthew 5:5), while the wicked don't.

Lastly, you cannot lose what you give away, and you cannot keep what you will not release. Indeed, a righteous resolve has a relentless trust in the Lord. Obedience, generosity and contentment all require tenacious trust. Therefore, resolve in your heart to go hard after God. Release your relentless pursuits, only after He has released you. Perhaps you ask, "Is my resolve righteous, or is it contingent on circumstances?"

The Bible says, "Alarmed, Jehoshaphat resolved to inquire of the Lord" (2 Chronicles 20:3).

Where do I need a righteous resolve to remain true to my commitment and calling?

Related Readings: Psalm 15:5; Daniel 1:8; Romans 8:35-39; 1 Corinthians 2:2

13

Possessions Complicate

Their possessions were so great that they were not able to stay together.
And quarreling arose...
Genesis 13:6b, 7a

Abram and Lot had a lot of stuff. They were blessed with family, friends and finances. However, things became complicated, and they were unable to coexist with each other. Though they needed one another, they could not stay together. The fear of losing their possessions superseded the joy of growing their relationship. So they divided, and as a result of their vulnerability, Lot lost everything. Jesus said, "A household divided against itself will not stand..." (Matthew 12:25).

Possessions are not wrong in themselves. However, when the management of your wealth compromises your loyalty to people, there is a problem. Possessions should be subservient to people, otherwise things get out of kilter. People know if you value your net worth over them. So how do we keep this balance between possessions and people?

Begin with an inventory of your time. How do you spend your time? Do you spend more time managing your stuff or loving on people? You may need to sell some of your property or, better yet, give it away. If your possessions have priority over people, there is a problem. Ask yourself, "Does my stuff compete with my relationship with God?" Perhaps you should downsize your stuff so you can upsize your focus on your Savior, Jesus.

By God's grace, use the material fortune He has entrusted to you as a magnet that draws you closer to God and people. Use your blessing of discretionary time to bless others.

The Bible says, "Command those who are rich in this present world not to be arrogant nor to put their hope in wealth, which is so uncertain, but to put their hope in God, who richly provides us with everything for our enjoyment. Command them to do good, to be rich in good deeds, and to be generous and willing to share. In this way they will lay up treasure for themselves as a firm foundation for the coming age, so that they may take hold of the life that is truly life" (1 Timothy 6:17-19).

How can I position my possessions so the Lord possesses more of me, and my family?

Related Readings: Genesis 36:6-7; Ecclesiastes 5:10-11; Luke 3:11; 2 Corinthians 9:6-15

14

Faithful Guide

The integrity of the upright guides them,
but the unfaithful are destroyed by their duplicity.
Proverbs 11:3

Integrity is an instrument of Almighty God. He uses it to guide His children in the direction He desires for them. Have you ever wondered what God would have you do? Integrity is His directive to do the next right thing, and trust Him with the results. It is out of our honesty we begin to comprehend Christ's desires. He delights in our uprightness.

For example, are you totally honest on your tax return? Is your tax preparer a person of unquestionable integrity? We can trust professionals to represent us well, but we are ultimately responsible for honest outcomes. Furthermore, is there anything you are doing, if printed as a newspaper headline, which would embarrass you and your family? Indeed, integrity brings joy to heaven and security on earth. It is your guide for godly living.

Moreover, the iniquity of the unfaithful destroys. The blessing of God is removed, as it cannot be bought with bad behavior. Relationships are scarred, and some are even severed over dishonest dealings. Overnight, poor judgment can soil and potentially destroy a hard-earned reputation. Pride makes a person think integrity is only for others. It deceives itself and becomes a disgrace for its dishonest and duplicitous ways. Iniquity is an unfaithful guide.

So we ask ourselves, "How can I be a man or woman of integrity over the balance of my life?" There is plainness about a person who bases their behavior on the principles of God's Word. Nothing fancy, only faithful living in your daily routine. The grace of God governs your soul, the truth of God renews your mind, and accountability is an anchor for your actions. Honestly ask yourself, "Is integrity my faithful guide?"

The Bible says, "May integrity and uprightness protect me, because my hope is in You" (Psalm 25:21).

How can I better integrate integrity as a guide for my business dealings and behavior at home?

Related Readings: Genesis 20:4-7; Hosea 13:9; Matthew 7:13; Romans 7:9-12

15

Faith Stretcher

"Abraham fell facedown; he laughed and said to himself, 'Will a son be born
to a man a hundred years old? Will Sarah bear a child at the age of ninety?'"
Genesis 17:17

Sometimes God's will is not logical or doesn't even seem possible. Abraham certainly struggled with the idea of being a parent as a centenarian and of his wife conceiving at ninety years of age. It wasn't possible; it didn't make sense. Yet in reality all things are possible with God, and this was one of them.

The Lord made a promise that was out of the ordinary. He wanted to mark this occasion with an indelible stamp of a "God thing." Abraham tried to give God a way around this miraculous method by offering Him another plan. However, God was not interested in another plan, He was interested in setting the stage for a blessing that would validate His sovereignty and that would take the faith of Abraham, Sarah and an entire nation to a whole other level. God wants us and He wants us to take Him at His word.

Why is it hard to take God at His word? Why do we struggle with believing in something that is not logical or that takes us out of our comfort zone? One reason we struggle is because of our perception of God. We make Him so small. We bring Him down to our level rather than allowing Him to pull us up to His level! This is man-centered thinking; instead, let's allow God to be God.

Faith allows us to travel places with God that we would never experience otherwise. Wouldn't you rather be in the middle of a lake in a storm with Jesus, than on the calm shore around a warm fire without Him? This is where faith trumps logic. We trust Him when it doesn't make sense; we follow Him when we are not sure of the destination.

We believe Him when others think we are strange, too religious or even fanatical. Let your Savior stretch your faith, and trust Him with the opportunity in front of you. Has your laughter turned to trust in God and awe of His accomplishments?

The Bible says, "Your father Abraham rejoiced to see My day, and he saw it and was glad" (John 8:56, NASB).

What impossibility am I facing that, with trust in God, becomes possible?

Related Readings: Deuteronomy 9:18-25; Psalm 126:1; Matthew 2:11; Romans 4:20

16

Benefits of Kindness

A kindhearted woman gains respect, but ruthless men gain only wealth.
A kind man benefits himself, but a cruel man brings trouble on himself.
Proverbs 11:16-17

Kindness benefits everyone. It brings joy to the giver, and peace to the receiver. The recipient reciprocates it, because respect is embedded in kindness. Kindheartedness facilitates respect, because it treats others with dignity and honor. Even when offended or ostracized, a gracious heart takes the higher ground of humility and gentleness. It may not be liked, but it is respected. Kind actions attract the Almighty's approval.

What is kindness? At its core it is a reflection of Christ. It is what we expect of the Lord when we desire good things. Listen to the heart of this employee's prayer for his boss to experience God's kindness in marriage, "O Lord, God of my master Abraham, give me success today, and show kindness to my master Abraham" (Genesis 24:12). In the same way your Savior shows you kindness both in salvation and in His severe mercy.

Furthermore, because of Christ's great kindness, you are compelled to compassionate actions. Ruthless men and women use whatever means of fear and intimidation to gain wealth and power, but considerate adults do not compromise their character for cash or influence. Indeed, God's great kindness grants us the favor we need. The Bible says, "The Lord was with him [Joseph]; he showed him kindness and granted him favor in the eyes of the prison warden" (Genesis 39:21).

Who doesn't need kindness? The undeserving especially needs your kindness, as a reminder of God's lasting love and infinite forgiveness. Be kind to the unkind, and they will see what really rests in your heart of hearts. Your kindheartedness will lead others to your source—Jesus Christ. Here the kindness of the Lord leads to repentance.

The Bible says, "Or do you show contempt for the riches of his kindness, tolerance and patience, not realizing that God's kindness leads you toward repentance?" (Romans 2:4).

Is there one who has been unkind to me to whom I can extend kindness?

Related Readings: Joshua 2:12; Ruth 3:10; Acts 4:9; Ephesians 2:6-8

17

Be a Blessing

So he [Jacob] went to him and kissed him.
When Isaac caught the smell of his clothes, he blessed him and said...
Genesis 27:27a

What is a blessing? It represents God's goodwill. Furthermore, He uses people as a channel for His blessing. It invokes divine favor, and confers well-being and prosperity to others. We all long for blessing. We desire blessing from God, and blessing from those we love and respect. This high level of approval and support comes in a variety of forms.

A blessing can be words of admonishment and instruction. It represents words that paint a larger context of God's overall will and purpose for your life. Blessings not only represent God's favor and direction, but they also sanction support from other servants of Christ. So, where does this longing to be blessed lead? It means you first receive the blessing of God and others so you in turn can be a blessing.

Think today, how you can be a blessing to another. How can you give people a divine context so they recognize and enjoy God's purpose in their life? Perhaps it is a quiet private prayer for them. Or, the Lord may lead you to publicly lay hands on someone, while asking for His blessing to reside on their life and work. Your bold blessing may be just what someone needs as they continue in their faithfulness to their family and faith. It can be a simple word of encouragement or a letter of gratitude.

Your blessing to others can be formal or informal. Think of creative ways to formally bless your children as they transition into adulthood, or how you can informally bless a friend launching into a new career. In Christ we bless others; without Christ we curse others. If we do nothing, people are prone to fill in the blank with negative thoughts and feelings. What power you have through the power of a blessing. Use it prayerfully and happily. Have you been blessed, so you can bless?

The Bible says, "Her children arise and call her blessed; her husband also, and he praises her..." (Proverbs 31:28).

Is there one I can bless today who may not feel worthy of a blessing?

Related Readings: Genesis 5:2; 2 Samuel 6:20; 1 Peter 3:9; Revelation 1:3

18

Forgiveness Heals

But Esau ran to meet Jacob and embraced him;
he threw his arms around his neck and kissed him. And they wept.
Genesis 33:4

Just like the prodigal son (whom Jesus describes in Luke 15) became broken and repentant, so does Jacob. Just as the loving father forgives, embraces and weeps with the son, so Esau does with Jacob. It is a beautiful, beautiful picture of forgiveness. Deception was overcome by forgiveness. Stealing was overcome by forgiveness. Hurt was overcome by forgiveness. Anger was overcome by forgiveness. Pride was overcome by forgiveness.

Running away was overcome by forgiveness. Coming back together was facilitated by forgiveness. Forgiveness through Christ and toward each other is the great reconciler. Otherwise, we live life like men and women most miserable, still blaming others and lamenting over injustice inflicted on us and those we love. It's not fair, because life hurts our idealism and optimism; however, to forgive is to be healed. So how do we forgive?

It begins with an encounter with God, as the originator of forgiveness embraces us. He is the one with limitless capacity to forgive. His forgiveness engulfs us with ability, a mandate and a reservoir of forgiveness. Because He has thoroughly forgiven us through Christ, we can and will forgive others for Christ's sake. It is the essence of being a Christian. If you are a Christian, you forgive.

Why is this hard? One reason is our immature faith lacks a cure. Our focus is still on our needs and hurts, but God is calling us to forgive. It is a faith place of loving Him and loving people. When you choose to live by faith, you forgive. When you forgive, you trust that God is working to make you, and others, more like Jesus. Begin today. Let God embrace you; you embrace another, and then watch forgiveness do its work.

The Bible says, "Therefore confess your sins to each other and pray for each other so that you may be healed" (James 5:16a).

Who is the one I can forgive today and begin the process of healing?

Related Readings: Psalm 30:2; Isaiah 53:5; Mark 5:34; 1 Peter 2:24

19

Destructive Jealousy

His brothers were jealous of him...
Genesis 37:11a

Jealousy bears the fruit of anger and criticism, as Joseph was the brunt of his brothers' envy. They did not appreciate his perceived disloyalty and his boastful attitude and actions. Joseph was very gifted and was held in high esteem by his father, but what should have worked to his advantage actually worked against him.

When another of greater influence likes you, you are set up to arouse the jealousy of others. If you are wise, you will discern this and seek to deflect unnecessary attention and accolades from a well-meaning leader. If you enjoy this, or take advantage of it by talking down to or behaving arrogantly toward others; you will only enrage an already smoldering fire of jealousy. Instead, spread the compliments and give the team credit.

A mature person will see jealousy coming and seek to preclude it by helping others be successful. For example, if you are given a position of influence, you will use this advantage for the benefit of others. Use your good will to spread the credit of success among the team. Downplay any of your accomplishments and shine the spotlight on the character and accomplishments of others.

However, even when you practice discretion and seek to serve others, there will still be a small room for jealousy. If someone chooses to reside in this small room, it is beyond your control. Only small people live in small rooms. Over time most people will recognize the smallness of others. It is their choice to grow up and join the team. Trust God with this person and situation. He will bring about His will, in His way, and in His time. Are you encouraging or discouraging jealousy?

The Bible says, "You are still worldly. For since there is jealousy and quarreling among you, are you not worldly? Are you not acting like mere men?" (1 Corinthians 3:3).

Do I need to let go of jealousy and replace it with gratitude?

Related Readings: 1 Samuel 18:1-3; Proverbs 27:4; Acts 13:45; 2 Corinthians 11:2

20

The Great Adventure

By faith Abraham, when called to go to a place he would later receive as his
inheritance, obeyed and went, even though he did not know where he was going.

Hebrews 11:8

God's will is a series of discoveries. And it is the transition between discoveries that
tests the true nature of my faith. I can press forward by faith or I can analyze the
situation until I am paralyzed by uncertainty. Abraham continued toward the unknown
because he was certain the Lord was leading him. Great adventure accompanies my
obedience to God.

Believers who are bound and determined to obey Christ are not bored. We are
compelled by the love for our Lord to conquer the next challenging circumstance and
to pioneer the unfamiliar in prayer. We become soft and satisfied when we stop
seeking out the next Kingdom opportunity. Our Savior Jesus is our Sherpa (guide), as
we travel on in trust. "He guides the humble in what is right and teaches them His
way" (Psalm 25:9).

Are you inspired or intimidated by your faith adventure? Do you anticipate or dread
doing the next right thing, as you fulfill God's calling on your life? Yes, Christ must come
to you in clarity before you go out for Him in obedience. But once you are sure of the
Lord's leading, do not let up until you have arrived at His destination. Go on your great
adventure with God and, like a visit to a new country, enjoy the new sites and people.

The Holy Spirit directs a life on the move, not one that is stuck, preoccupied with either
pleasure or pain. "A man's heart plans his way, but the Lord directs his steps"
(Proverbs 16:9). So, make prayerful plans, but all the while remain nimble to the nudge
of God's Spirit. If you fall in love with your plans, you may miss adjusting to the
Almighty's way.

There is a reward to those who remain true to God's call. It may only be the satisfaction of knowing you faithfully followed the Lord, but this is all that matters in the end.
As a pilgrim passing through this life, launch your next eternal endeavor and

experience the righteous ride with Him. Nothing risked may mean nothing lost, but every journey for Jesus is great gain. Discover what He wants today, and it will lead to what He wants tomorrow.

What great adventure does God have for me? What can I do today to trust and obey?

Related Readings: Proverbs 11:3; Isaiah 48:17; Luke 4:1-3; Galatians 5:16-18

21

Refreshers Are Refreshed

A generous man will prosper;
he who refreshes others will himself be refreshed.
Proverbs 11:25

What does it mean to refresh? It is to be made fresh, to revive, enliven, invigorate, rejuvenate, energize, restore, recharge or revitalize. A meager cup of lukewarm coffee comes alive with taste and satisfaction, when mixed with freshly brewed beans. A lukewarm life is warmed and encouraged, when refreshed with words of encouragement and acts of kindness. Everyone we meet become a candidate for refreshment.

Our faith cools down when Christ seems silent and circumstances continue to crumble, but a sincere prayer from a righteous friend restores and warms our confidence. Our hope feels deferred in the face of disappointment and rejection, but we are energized by the acceptance and love of a community of believers in Jesus. Hope loves company. Seek refreshment from your Savior and His followers. Be refreshed, so you can refresh others.

When your parched soul has been watered by dew from heaven, you can lead others to the Lord's watering hole. People are frantic from feeling robbed by insensitive institutions and greedy governments, but we can reconnect them to their generous God. Jesus gives us an abundant life to be shared with others with an absence of abundance. "I have come that they may have life, and that they may have it more abundantly" (John 10:10b).

Lastly, your refreshment reciprocates refreshment. When you refresh another financially, you are refreshed by faith and fulfillment. When you refresh another emotionally, you are refreshed by peace and contentment. When you refresh another spiritually, you are refreshed by the grace and love of God. Are you in need of refreshment? If so, receive Christ's full cup of joy. Drink often with the Lord, so you can generously refresh friends.

The Bible says, "Taste and see that the LORD is good; blessed is the man who takes refuge in him" (Psalm 34:8).

How can I stay in a routine of refreshment, so I in turn can refresh others?

Related Readings: Ruth 2:14; Psalm 41:1; Matthew 25:34-35; 2 Corinthians 9:6-7

22

False Trust

Whoever trusts in his riches will fall,
but the righteous will thrive like a green leaf.
Proverbs 11:28

Trust in stuff will cause you to stumble, and eventually fall. Why? Why is money unfit for trust? It is unreliable because it cannot save us or bring us forgiveness, peace or contentment. Money is an unemotional master that can trip you up if it becomes the basis for your security. It can be here today and gone tomorrow. Money moves around like a gypsy looking for the next place to live. Trust in riches takes the focus off Christ.

The Bible says, "Cast but a glance at riches, and they are gone, for they will surely sprout wings and fly off to the sky like an eagle" (Proverbs 23:5). Trust in riches causes some to fall from the faith because they equate wealth with success. However, you can be faithful to the Lord, and thus be successful whether rich or poor. It may take us losing money to reveal our true motivations. Trust in riches is a recipe for false security, fear and sadness.

However, the righteous understands the role of riches is to remind them of God's provision. The Bible says, "Moreover, when God gives any man wealth and possessions, and enables him to enjoy them, to accept his lot and be happy in his work—this is a gift of God" (Ecclesiastes 5:19). Are you struggling with the reduction of your wealth? Remember your first job—what really mattered? Was it trust in the Lord, your parents and good health? The righteous thrive in trust and obedience to Christ.

Lastly, guard your good name during a financial crisis. Character is of much greater value than cash. The Bible says, "A good name is more desirable than great riches; to be esteemed is better than silver or gold" (Proverbs 22:1)." This means you don't fear, and you follow through with your commitments. Faith grows in its giving during uncertain times.

Am I thriving or surviving? Is my trust in gold or God?

Related Readings: Deuteronomy 8:12-14; Job 31:24-25; Matthew 13:22; 1 Timothy 6:17

23

Unpretentious Living

Better to be a nobody and yet have a servant than
pretend to be somebody and have no food.
Proverbs 12:9

Unpretentious living is an invitation to down-to-earth interaction with others. Rest and relaxation attend to those who are truly themselves, without acting like someone they're not. However, pretentious speech and behavior require extra energy to engage with their environment. Contentment is illusive and intimacy is an illusion. I become the most stressed when I feel I have to live up to something, or be someone I'm not.

Moreover, when you are real and not fake, your friends feel the freedom to do the same. You give off energy, instead of forever sucking it from others. I have to be honest and ask often, "Am I being myself, or am I trying to dress, talk, drive a certain car, or live in a high-status neighborhood that is motivated by a need to be somebody I'm not?" Pretense is birthed out of pride, but humility is the fruit of unpretentious living.

Jesus is clear, "For everyone who exalts himself will be humbled, and he who humbles himself will be exalted" (Luke 14:11 NASB). In Christ you are somebody. High or low net worth, small or large home, new or used car, prestigious university or common college, in Him you are somebody. You are somebody to your Savior Jesus.

The Bible says, "Christ in you, the hope of glory" (Colossians 1:27b). Out of your simple faith and modesty, the Lord takes center stage of your life. Humility positions you to point people to heaven. Therefore, keep your life unencumbered, so people can see your Savior shine forth. Ask yourself, "Whom am I trying to impress, people I really don't know, or the Lover of my soul, Jesus?"

The Bible says, "Those who want to make a good impression outwardly are trying to compel you to be circumcised. The only reason they do this is to avoid being persecuted for the cross of Christ" (Galatians 6:12).

How can I be more authentic and open with my spouse, children and work associates?

Related Readings: 1 Samuel 16:7; Proverbs 13:7; Romans 2:28; 1 Peter 3:3

24

Routine Work

He who works his land will have abundant food,
but he who chases fantasies lacks judgment.
Proverbs 12:11

Routine work may not be sexy, but it is necessary. It is necessary to meet our needs and the needs of those who depend on us. The same work day in and day out can seem simple and even boring, but it is a test of our faithfulness. Will I continue to faithfully carry out uncomplicated responsibilities, even when my attention span is suffering? If so, this is God's path to blessing, "Steady plodding brings prosperity..."(Proverbs 21:5, TLB).

The contrast to routine work is chasing after phantom deals that are figments of our imagination. Be careful not to be led astray by fantasies that lead nowhere. It is false faith to think a gimmick or some conniving circumstance can replace hard work. Wisdom stops chasing after the next scheme and sticks instead to the certainty of available work. What do your parents say is the smart thing to do? Give them all the facts and listen.

Furthermore, work is easily carried out when everything is going well, and there are no indicators of job loss or an increase in responsibilities with less pay. However, it is during these uncertain times that Christ followers can step up and set the example. Your attitudes of hope and hard work are a testimony of trust in the Lord. Stay engaged in executing your tasks with excellence, and you will inspire others to their labor of love.

Lastly, see routine work as your worship of the Lord. He is blessing your faithfulness to follow through with the smallest of details. Are you content to serve Christ in your current career? The Bible says, "Whatever you do, work at it with all your heart, as working for the Lord, not for men, since you know that you will receive an inheritance from the Lord as a reward. It is the Lord Christ you are serving" (Colossians 3:23-24).

How can I be a compelling example for Christ during my routine work?

Related Readings: Genesis 2:15; 1 Kings 19:19; Romans 12:11; 1 Timothy 4:11-12

Follow Jesus First

"When Jesus saw the crowd around him, he gave orders to cross to
the other side of the lake. Then a teacher of the law came to him and said,
'Teacher, I will follow you wherever you go.'"
Matthew 8:18-19

Good leaders are first good followers. Do you follow the orders of Jesus? When He asks you to do the uncomfortable, do you move out of your comfort zone with confidence? Compelling Christian leadership has focused "followship" on their Master, the Lord Jesus. Where is He asking you to go that requires sacrifice and unconditional commitment? His orders do not always make sense, but they are totally trustworthy and helpful.

When He directs you to leave the noise of the crowds to the quietness of a few, do not delay. If you are obsessed by activity, you can easily lose your edge on energy and faith. When all my oomph is consumed on serving every request and answering every call, I have no time or concentration to hear from Christ. What is He saying? This is the most important inquiry I can make. What is Jesus telling me to do? So, when I listen, I learn.

You may be in the middle of a monster season of success, so make sure your achievements do not muffle the Lord's message. It's when we are fast and furious that our faith becomes perfunctory and predictable. Leadership requires alone time to retool and recalibrate our character. People follow when they know you've been with Jesus.

The most difficult part may be the transition from doing less, to listening and thinking more. If you as the leader are not planning ahead, who is? Who has the best interests of the enterprise in mind? Who is defending the mission and vision of the organization, so there is not a drift into competing strategies? Follow Jesus first; then He frees you to see.

Where is the Lord leading you to go? Will you lag behind with excellent excuses, or will you make haste and move forward by faith? Go with God and He will direct you through the storms of change. He may seem silent at times, but remember, He led you to this place, and where He leads, He provides. Follow Jesus first, and go wherever He goes.

You will lose people in the process, but you will gain better people for His next phase.

"Then Jesus said to his disciples, 'If anyone would come after me, he must deny himself and take up his cross and follow me'" (Matthew 16:24).

Where is Jesus leading me to go? Am I willing to let go and trust Him with what's next?

Related Readings: Numbers 32:11; Isaiah 8:10-12; 1 Corinthians 1:11-13; Revelation 14:4

26

Diligence Rules

Diligent hands will rule, but laziness ends in slave labor.
Proverbs 12:24

How hard do you work, or do you hardly work? God said to Adam, "Cursed is the ground because of you; through painful toil you will eat of it all the days of your life.... By the sweat of your brow you will eat your food" (Genesis 3:17b, 19a). And He explained to Moses, "Six days you shall labor and do all your work, but the seventh day is a Sabbath to the Lord your God. On it you shall not do any work..." (Exodus 20:9-10a).

Has our culture become accustomed to receiving good things without great effort? Who is entitled to influence without being industrious? Perhaps there is a dearth of diligence that has depressed people and economies. Laziness leads to the control of others, while honest labor is given opportunities and advancement. Do not despair in your diligence, for you are set up for success. Mind your business meticulously, and you will enjoy the business.

Indeed, intense industry leads to preferment. The Bible says, "Now the man Jeroboam was a valiant warrior, and when Solomon saw that the young man was industrious, he appointed him over all the forced labor of the house of Joseph" (1 Kings 11:28 NASB). Your faithfulness to your work is not going unnoticed. Your diligence is a distinctive that separates you from the average or lazy laborer. Security comes with this level of service.

Lastly, the Lord blesses hands that are hard at work. He smiles when He sees your service exceeds expectations. You go the extra mile to make sure others are cared for, just as you would like to be treated. God knows because of your thoroughness on the job, and your integrity in its execution, you can be trusted with more.

The Bible says, "The elders who direct the affairs of the church well are worthy of double honor, especially those whose work is preaching and teaching" (1 Timothy 5:17).

What does my hard work look like when it is done for the Lord?

Related Readings: 1 Kings 12:20; Proverbs 10:4; Romans 12:8; 1 Timothy 4:15

27

Righteous Hatred

The righteous hate what is false,
but the wicked bring shame and disgrace.
Proverbs 13:5

There is a righteous hatred that rejects what is false. It might be false words, bogus behavior, a counterfeit countenance, a phony friendship or deceptive dealings. The discernment of the Spirit-filled believer rises up to defend integrity. You can't sit still in the face of shenanigans when you know there is a violation of an agreed upon code of ethics.

So, how are we to respond to lies and liars? We first look in the mirror and make sure we are honest in our dealings and accurate with our words. Jesus said, "How can you say to your brother, 'Let me take the speck out of your eye,' when all the time there is a plank in your own eye?" (Matthew 7:4). It's required I remove all self-deception before I can clearly see sin in another brother. Self-evaluation precedes confronting false conduct.

Furthermore, our Heavenly Father expresses holy hatred over what's false. He hates "haughty eyes, a lying tongue...a heart that devises wicked schemes" (Proverbs 6:17a, 18a). Because the Almighty abhors artificial acts, we must ask ourselves, "Do I take sin seriously or do I casually flirt with it?" Loose lips lead to lies and deceit that bring shame and embarrassment. Avoid lies and liars, and you will live in peace and contentment.

Lastly, in your business, ministry and testimony, remove all appearance of fraud and falsehood. Free yourself from image management with full disclosure and transparency. Create a culture that exposes any hint of a conflict of interest. Lies examined under light melt away. Hate dishonesty and reward honesty. Honesty is the only policy for the people of God.

The Bible says, "Therefore each of you must put off falsehood and speak truthfully to his neighbor, for we are all members of one body" (Ephesians 4:25).

How can I take more seriously what the Lord hates in order to honor Him?

Related Readings: Judges 16:11; Psalm 119:163; Colossians 3:9; Revelation 21:8

28

Faith Versus Fear

"He replied, 'You of little faith, why are you so afraid?'
Then he got up and rebuked the winds and the waves, and it was completely calm."
Matthew 8:26

Jesus responds to little faith or large faith. They are both important to Him. However, the larger your faith grows the smaller your fears shrink. And the opposite is true. The smaller your faith, the greater your fears. It may seem like Jesus is asleep as you are riding out this particular storm. He doesn't seem to care or be in control. However, during hard days like these, we ask ourselves, "Is God big enough to handle my greatest fear?"

Some of your peers may not believe like you believe, but they certainly need to believe that you really do believe in what you believe. It is during these adversarial times they see your faith validated. Your faith during this storm may be what draws someone to Jesus. Your peace and comfort is appealing and appetizing. This is what the human soul hungers and longs for. Your trust in God is required to calmly endure this crisis of belief.

Furthermore, untested faith can be weak underneath. Weak faith is a little faith. A new Christian may be passionate and on fire. Gratitude floods their soul, but this enthusiasm will be short lived without shoring up a weaker faith. Emotional faith can be a bridge to a closer walk with Jesus. Your feelings can stir your heart to receive eternal truth. A life storm awakens you to a fresh need for Jesus, so use this awareness to grow your faith.

Lastly, the stronger your faith grows, the weaker your fears become. It is imperative for you to feed your faith and to starve your fears. Feast on the Bible, for a promise a day keeps fear away. Truth fosters faith. If the cancer of fear has infected the bone marrow of your faith, let the Lord do a truth transfusion. Jesus is here for you. He will calm the storm, but in the meantime trust Him. Watch your faith grow and your fears melt away.

The Bible says, "God is our refuge and strength, an ever-present help in trouble. Therefore we will not fear..." (Psalm 46:1-2a).

What one fear do I need to replace with faith in Jesus?

Related Readings: Psalm 91:5; Isaiah 54:4; Roman 8:15; 1 Peter 3:6

29

Skill and Ability

See I have chosen Bezalel... and I have filled him with the Spirit of God,
with skill, ability and knowledge in all kinds of crafts...
Exodus 31:2a, 3

Our ability to work comes from God. Our ability to earn a degree and make money comes from God. Our ability to paint, sing, play a musical instrument and execute a deal, they all come from God. He calls us and He equips us to carry out His will for our lives. Where He calls; He equips. And yes, if you do not use the God-given abilities you have, you could lose them.

You could lose them because of poor stewardship or a bad testimony. You could lose your skills because of atrophy. Just as muscle shrinks and becomes useless without use; so do the skills, abilities, gifts and knowledge given to us by God. How are you doing in the management of your God-given abilities? His expectations are for you to continue to grow and improve. He wants you to focus on the things you do the very best.

As we mature, ideally we narrow our focus to the one thing that is effortless for us. The one thing that others say we do best and that blesses them when they are around us. Position your life to do the one thing that you have become a genius at doing by God's grace. It may be teaching; then focus on teaching. It may be leading; then focus on leading. It may be coaching; then focus on coaching. It may be singing; then focus on singing. It may be parenting; then focus on parenting. It may be writing; then focus on writing.

This requires discipline and in some cases sacrifice, but trust God with who you are. Serve out of your sweet spot, so you and everyone around you will be blessed. Yes, there are economic considerations, but each stage of life has its own opportunities. Stay nimble and seize each opportunity in the context of what you do best, and never forget to give God the credit for your abilities.

The Bible says, "Therefore I remind you to stir up the gift of God which is in you through the laying on of my hands" (2 Timothy 1:6, NKJV).

How can I better steward my God-given skills and abilities for His glory?

Related Readings: Deuteronomy 33:11; Proverbs 22:29; John 3:27; 1 Corinthians 12:4-11

30

Dollar Cost Averaging

Dishonest money dwindles away,
but he who gathers money little by little makes it grow.
Proverbs 13:11

Is there a method to your money management? Do you have a process in place to steadily save over time? If not, it is never too late to set up a system for saving. Some of us struggle with this, because we bet on big returns only to suffer loss. Steadily saving is not sexy but secure. Finances can be an elusive enemy or a friend who has our back.

Get-rich-quick schemes only feed greed. In God's economy it is the one who diligently deposits smaller amounts in a secure place who reaps rewards. It is wise wealth that makes the first 10% of their income a gift offering in the form of a tithe to their Heavenly Father and the second 10% an investment in their future. Money obtained by vanity is spent on vanity, but money gained by hard work and honesty is retained for growth.

It does take discipline to not spend all our earnings in an instant. Advertising and our obligation as consumers exploit our emotions. Culture sucks us in to spend not all we have but more than we have, so be on guard with a simple system for savings. For example, set up an automatic draft from each paycheck that goes straight into a savings account. Preserve this cash, and one day your financial fruit tree will become an orchard.

Lastly, look to the Lord as your provider and see yourself as a steward of His stuff. The management of your Master's money requires savings. God's desire is growth in your financial security, so you are free to give more and serve others.

The Bible says, "The plans of the diligent lead to profit as surely as haste leads to poverty" (Proverbs 21:5).

Am I frivolously spending just for today, or am I disciplined each day to deposit a dollar toward tomorrow?

Related Readings: Psalm 128:2; Jeremiah 17:11; Ephesians 4:28; James 5:1-5

N O T E S

WHAT READERS ARE SAYING
ABOUT WISDOM HUNTERS

Thank you so much for sharing this specific article. It was truly speaking to me. I have been crying and praying, when I woke up The Lord directed me straight to this email and I had to read it twice! It was on time! The Lord used it along with the scripture you shared to speak volumes into my spirt for renewed strength. Thank you so much and may God continue to bless you and give strength to do His work. In Him, Tracey

I want to thank you for your devotion this morning regarding identity. I truly needed that. I was widowed 21 years ago and finished raising my kids, went back to school and have the work I love. But I had just kept taking on more and more till I had to cut back and ask, "why". I began to realize I was finding my identity in what I did instead of who I am in Christ. Even though I work for a church denomination and speak around the world. It scared me. How and where did I lose sight of what is really what it is all about. Running here, flying there, projects in Africa, and training women to be all they can be in Christ. I was doing right things and telling others how to do it but began to realize I was empty inside, wor n out, and deeply longing for Jesus to sweep me away. I was needing to reconnect on a deeper level than ever before. I have even longed a few times for that devastating time of losing my husband suddenly, to put me back into that perspective of God's loving arms around me; a time when I felt so helpless and totally dependent on Him. That time of relying so deep and complete. A time when taking one breath at a time seemed overwhelming. God held me in His loving arms no matter how sad or angry or hopeless I felt. Today, I am asking God to fill me and let me rest and find myself totally in Him again, even deeper. Bless you for your words this morning. They made me realize "In Him only shalt thou stand". - Mary Jo

I have always enjoyed your wonderful insights to daily living along with the struggles it may bring. Thank you so much for sharing your life with us on such a personal level. You are right when you say that you ARE important to Christ. We cannot let the world tell us otherwise…no matter what! God bless you and keep you close to Him. Regards, - Jimmy

God spoke to me through this devotional today. I am an active 'listener' and have sought God's patience, direction, and guidance when listening to others. It is challenging because I had to accept that my role, in many relationships, is to listen.....and not be listened to. Once I accepted this as God's path for me, I gave Him my frustration/resentment over not being listened to and it has opened up a new closeness between God and I because He ALWAYS listens!! Thank you so much for this devotional because God used it to affirm my 'listening ear'.
– Heather

I'm printing this one off! What a beautiful reminder. I can't tell you how much these daily devotionals continually help me to stop, focus and pray. Each day my intentions are good to spend in quiet time but then I start with the newspaper, check my email and I'm off. But then I see "Wisdom" and it reminds me to STOP! Know that God is using you and your devotionals in ways you can't believe!! Thank you for your gift!!! – Julie

Mr. Bailey, I just want to thank you for your work. Your daily devotionals have helped me so much. So many times I am struggling with one issue or another and your devotional will speak straight to my heart, soul and mind and give me the answers I am desperately searching for. You are a wonderful blessing in my life as well as many others. -- Leticia

Totally needed to see this today. Been striving in my thinking, wondering what's next in my faith walk as I get to the end of this current season of paying off my debt. God has been encouraging me to rest in His good plans and purposes for me. Even though I cannot see exactly what's next, I can trust in the One who is in control of it. – Joanna

Thank you, God used this email to yet again, shake me, and set me straight in my walk with Him. Please don't ever get discouraged. Your ministry is truly your calling. May God continue to bless you and the ministry. – Krystal

BECOMING A DISCIPLE
OF JESUS CHRIST

My journey that led me to God covered a span of 19 years, before I truly understood my need for His love and forgiveness in a personal relationship with Jesus Christ. Along this path of spiritual awakening, God placed many people along the way as spiritual guideposts directing me toward Him.

Initially it was my mother who took me to church at age 12 so I could learn about faith through the confirmation process. My grandmother was a role model in her walk with Jesus by being kind and generous to all she encountered. Once in college, I began attending church with Rita (my future wife) and her family.

It was then that relevant weekly teaching from an ancient book—the Bible—began to answer many of life's questions. It intrigued me: What is God's plan for my life? Who is Jesus Christ? What are sin, salvation, heaven and hell? How can I live an - abundant life of forgiveness, joy and love?

So, the Lord found me first with His incredible love and when I surrendered in repentance and faith in Jesus, I found Him. For two years a businessman in our church showed me how to grow in grace through Bible study, prayer, faith sharing and service to others. I still discover each day more of God's great love and His new mercies.

Below is an outline for finding God and becoming a disciple of Jesus:

1. BELIEVE: "If you declare with your mouth, "Jesus is Lord," and believe in your heart that God raised him from the dead, you will be saved" (Romans 10:9). Belief in Jesus Christ as your Savior and Lord gives you eternal life in heaven.

2. REPENT AND BE BAPTIZED: "Peter replied, 'Repent and be baptized, every one of you, in the name of Jesus Christ for the forgiveness of your sins. And you will receive the gift of the Holy Spirit'" (Acts 2:38). Repentance means you turn from your sin and publically confess Christ in baptism.

3. OBEY: "Jesus replied, 'Anyone who loves me will obey my teaching. My Father will love them, and we will come to them and make our home with them'" (John 14:23). Obedience is an indicator of our love for the Lord Jesus and His presence in our life.

4. WORSHIP, PRAYER, COMMUNITY, EVANGELISM AND STUDY: "Every day they continued to meet together in the temple courts. They broke bread in their homes and ate together with glad and sincere hearts, praising God and enjoying the favor of all the people. And the Lord added to their number daily those who were being saved" (Acts 2:46-47). Worship and prayer are our expressions of gratitude and honor to God and our dependence on His grace. Community and evangelism are our accountability to Christians and compassion for non-Christians. Study to apply the knowledge, understanding, and wisdom of God.

5. LOVE GOD: "Jesus replied: 'Love the Lord your God with all your heart and with all your soul and with all your mind.' This is the first and greatest commandment" (Matthew 22:37-38). Intimacy with the almighty God is a growing and loving relationship. We are loved by Him, so we can love others and be empowered by the Holy Spirit to obey His commands.

6. LOVE PEOPLE: "And the second is like it: 'Love your neighbor as yourself'" (Matthew 22:39). Loving people is an outflow of the love for our heavenly Father. We are able to love because He first loved us.

7. MAKE DISCIPLES: "And the things you have heard me say in the presence of many witnesses entrust to reliable people who will also be qualified to teach others" (2 Timothy 2:2). The reason we disciple others is because we are extremely grateful to God and to those who disciple us, and we want to obey Christ's last instructions before going to heaven.

MEET THE AUTHOR

Boyd Bailey

Boyd Bailey, the author of Wisdom Hunters devotionals, is the founder of Wisdom Hunters, Inc., an Atlanta-based ministry created to encourage Christians (a.k.a wisdom hunters) to *apply God's unchanging Truth in a changing world.*

By God's grace, Boyd has impacted wisdom hunters in over 86 countries across the globe through the Wisdom Hunters daily devotion, wisdomhunters.com devotional blog and devotional books.

For over 30 years Boyd Bailey has passionately pursued wisdom through his career in fulltime ministry, executive coaching, and mentoring.

Since becoming a Christian at the age of 19, Boyd begins each day as a wisdom hunter, diligently searching for Truth in scripture, and through God's grace, applying it to his life.

These raw, 'real time' reflections from his personal time with the Lord, are now impacting over 111,000 people through the Wisdom Hunters Daily Devotion email. In addition to the daily devotion, Boyd has authored nine devotional books: *Infusion,* a 90-day devotional, *Seeking Daily the Heart of God Vol I & II,* 365-day devotionals *Seeking God in the Proverbs,* a 90-day devotional and *Seeking God in the Psalms,* a 90-day devotional along with several 30-day devotional e-Books on topics such as *Wisdom for Fathers, Wisdom for Mothers, Wisdom for Graduates,* and *Wisdom for Marriage.*

In addition to Wisdom Hunters, Boyd is the co-founder and CEO of Ministry Ventures, a faith based non-profit, where he has trained and coached over 1000 ministries in the best practices of prayer, board, ministry models, administration and fundraising. Prior to Ministry Ventures, Boyd was the National Director for Crown Financial Ministries and an Associate Pastor at First Baptist Church of Atlanta. Boyd serves on numerous boards including Ministry Ventures, Wisdom Hunters, Atlanta Mission, Souly Business and Blue Print for Life.

Boyd received his Bachelor of Arts from Jacksonville State University and his Masters of Divinity from Southwestern Seminary. He and Rita, his wife of 30 plus years, live in Roswell, Georgia and are blessed with four daughters, three sons-in-law who love Jesus, two granddaughters and two grandsons. Boyd and Rita enjoy missions and investing in young couples, as well as hiking, reading, traveling, working through their bucket list, watching college football, and hanging out with their kids and grand kids when ever possible.

Made in the USA
Charleston, SC
19 January 2015